"Did I Ever Tell You About When Your Grandparents Were Young?"

Deborah Shaw Lewis and Gregg Lewis

ZondervanPublishingHouse
Grand Rapids, Michigan

A Division of HarperCollins*Publishers*

"Did I Ever Tell You About When Your Grandparents Were Young?"
Copyright © 1994 by Deborah Shaw Lewis and Gregg Lewis

Zondervan Publishing House
Grand Rapids, Michigan 49530

Library of Congress Cataloging-in-Publication Data

Lewis, Deborah Shaw, 1951–
   "Did I ever tell you about when your grandparents were young?" : building
togetherness and values by sharing stories about your family / by Deborah Shaw
Lewis and Gregg Lewis.
   p. cm. — (Family share together book)
  ISBN 0-310-42121-7 (softcover)
  1. Family—Anecdotes. 2. Grandparents—Anecdotes. 3. Storytelling. 4. Family—
Folklore. 5. Oral biography. I. Lewis, Gregg A. II. Title. III. Series: Lewis,
Deborah Shaw, 1951– Family share-together book.
HQ518.L4824 1994
306.85—dc20
94-32863
CIP

Illustrations by Liz Conrad

Printed in the United States of America

94 95 96 97 98 99 / ❖ CH / 6 5 4 3 2 1

Welcome to the Adventure of Storytelling!

My husband Gregg admits that he never felt particularly close to his grandpa Lewis when he was a kid. Grandpa always seemed kind of gruff—never physically affectionate. Though Gregg's family visited the farm at least a couple of times every year, he and his brothers spent almost all their time with their cousins, doing chores or staging corncob wars in the barn.

Somehow, Gregg's feelings toward Grandpa changed. Gregg thinks it began when he was in college and took a summer job in Michigan near his farm. He occasionally drove to Grandma's and Grandpa's for a visit. Those were the first times he saw his grandparents on his own, as an adult.

Gregg's respect for his grandpa grew during his grandma's courageous, but futile two-year battle with cancer. He saw the rough man who'd spent a lifetime at hard labor become the most patient and gentle of nurses. Day and night his grandpa cared for the woman who had borne him four sons and had shared six decades of life with him.

A few weeks after his grandma died Gregg drove back to Michigan by himself to spend a few days with his grandpa. Grandpa would fix Gregg breakfast each morning, and then they would talk for a while about Grandpa's life, his marriage, and about Grandma. One day Grandpa told Gregg a story he'd never forget:

"It happened in the final months of your grandma's life—just before we had to put her in the nursing home," Grandpa said. "She'd gotten so weak she couldn't make it to the bathroom by herself. I had to carry her twenty times a day some days. There were many times she couldn't remember why she'd wanted to go, or what we were doing there. Eventually she reached the point where she lost control of her bodily functions altogether.

"One day I carried her to the bathroom to clean her up. As I was finishing the chore she spoke up as clear as day. 'Daddy, do you love me?' she asked. I kinda snorted in surprise to hear her say anything. And without even looking up at her I said, 'Do you think I'd be doing this if I didn't?' But that wasn't good enough for your grandma. She asked, 'But do you really love me?' So I stopped right

in the middle of what I was doing, stood up, and put my arms around her. And I said, 'Of course, I love you. You oughta know that by now.' She looked right into my eyes, smiled a big smile, and said, 'I know. But I just need to hear you say it.' "

Gregg told me, "Grandpa's story brought tears to my eyes. And it said more to me about love and commitment in marriage than any book I've every read or any sermon I've ever heard on the subject."

My own fondest memories regarding my husband's grandfather are of his stories. When Gregg and I first married, Grandpa was seventy-nine years old. He seemed much younger. Grandpa cut his own firewood and wore out several chainsaws after he turned seventy. When we would visit, he would sit in his favorite chair and tell one story after another.

Grandpa's gone now. He died at the age of ninety-four. But when we get together with Gregg's cousins for a weekend family reunion each August, we sit around and recount Grandpa's stories. And we agree: we all looked forward to those visits with Grandpa in his old Michigan farmhouse—especially the stories and the lessons we learned from them. And our appreciation for his storytelling grows.

Today as we look ahead to the twenty-first century, our culture is so youth-oriented we often forget the value of age. We find it difficult to remember that in years past, young people depended on parents and grandparents to hand down the practical information needed to succeed as adults. Farmers taught their sons how to be farmers; hunters taught their children the skills they needed to hunt. Even young people who sought a trade different from their parents', usually learned that trade from an older person. So, historically, as the elders of any culture aged and became less able to do things, their experience and wisdom became more valuable.

With the advent of fast-changing technology, however, each generation turns, not to the previous generation for life-skills, but to outside instruction. As a result, parents and grandparents who have spent a lifetime accumulating knowledge suddenly find much of their information is out of date.

Now, my father-in-law has his son set his electronic watch. My own mother bought her first computer when she was in her sixties, but she looks to my brothers to help her when she has problems with it. Most of us work with the high-tech necessities of our times—from home security systems to programmable VCRs—about which our parents and grandparents know very little. So today, as a person grows older, not only do his physical abilities wane, but his practical knowledge regarding our contemporary world also seems less relevant.

In the past, as a natural part of the process of their teaching practical, day-to-day skills to younger generations, elders also imparted the lessons and truths of their "life wisdom"—including an ability to make sense of life, to establish a personal identity, to feel connected to others, to appreciate the cycle of life with its highs and lows, and to embrace tested and lasting moral, spiritual, and societal values. But today, as we have turned away from our elders for the practical, day-to-day knowledge, we have also forgotten them as a resource of this "life wisdom." And in a world fast accelerating up the on-ramp of tomorrow's information super-highway, wisdom is one thing we are sadly lacking.

When we turn to the elders in our life for stories, we not only rediscover their wisdom, but the stories also serve another purpose. Psychologists call it "life review." Storytelling is one means by which older people weave together the events of their lives into a tapestry that integrates past and present. This pulling together of memories gives their lives meaning and validation. And in telling their stories, many elders can recognize their own impact on the world around them—the role they played in God's design.

When the stories are about our families, told by our grandparents, they reinforce our sense of family identity, bolster the self-esteem of both listener and teller, and define our personal and family values. From such stories, younger generations can sometimes absorb life's most important lessons. As they listen they learn how their grandparents grew up, conquered problems, moved to new places and made new lives, or resolved conflicts. As children hear the stories of success and failure, laughter and tears, courage and fear, from and about their grandparents, they gain the confidence that they, too, can overcome difficulties and find happiness—that they, too, have a place in God's design. At the same time, through the same stories, grandparents can rediscover their unique place in life and in the family.

Maybe you are a grandparent reading this and thinking, "I'm

no storyteller. My grandchildren won't want to hear about my life. Nothing interesting ever happened to me!"

Or perhaps you're reading this book as a member of a younger generation and you're thinking, "No one tells family stories in our family. I don't even know how to get my grandparents talking about their memories."

Then keep reading—for the rest of this book will be especially helpful for anyone of any generation interested in beginning or just enriching a family storytelling tradition. For while many grandparents will never be great storytellers, all grandparents have many stories their children and grandchildren will want to hear—and some they *need* to hear.

How do we uncover those stories? It may help to think of the memory as a computer. To call up information from our mind, we must first find the right file and a key word to access that file. Or we can think of our memories as a sprawling house, built by a creative contractor who simply added rooms as they were needed. Rediscovering memories is like walking down the twisting, turning hallways of that home and seeing closed doors in every direction.

In the pages that follow, our "Story Starters" and "Storytelling Tips" include a hodgepodge, bushel-basket full of story-triggering questions, suggestions, and comments to consider. The questions are designed for grandparents to ask themselves, or for children or grandchildren to ask grandparents. You might want to think of them as a computer menu for calling up old memory files, or as a set of keys to use to unlock the doors of a rambling house of recollections.

It's important to remember that some entries on a computer menu are seldom used. A few keys on our old key rings no longer open any doors. In the same way, not all of the ideas in this book will effectively trigger a memory from every grandparent. But some of them will. And when they do, there you will find a starting place for your own adventure of family storytelling.

Whether you are a grandparent yourself, or a child or grand-child wanting to get a grandparent storytelling tradition started in your family, we trust you'll find plenty of questions, suggestions, and samples here to help the members of your family discover, explore, and appreciate your own unique family heritage.

Tell about the first house you remember living in.

- When you think of that house, what's the first scene you picture in your mind?
- Name all the people who lived in that house with you.
- Do you remember the address or phone number?
- What did the house smell like and look like?
- Was this house in town or on a farm?
- Describe life on that farm.
- Why did you move and how old were you?
- What do you remember about other houses you lived in?
- What foods or smells do you associate with each house?

> *In our mind's computer, many of our memories are filed by the places in which they occurred. Remembering places is a powerful way to unlock the doors of our minds. As we talk about a place in our past, often the memories of events and people associated with that place will flow, as if a door has been opened. Out of those places and details, stories may grow.*

*If you could pick one day
that you could live over again,
just for the joy of being able to
experience it a second time,
what day would you pick?*

- How old were you?
- Tell everything you remember happening that day.
- Who else was there?
- Now, if you could pick one day that you could live over again and be able to change what you did that day—or change something that happened that day—what day would you pick? Tell us about it.

Listening to the experts can help you improve your own storytelling skills. We enjoy listening to tapes of great storytellers from the National Storytelling Association (P.O. Box 309, Jonesborough, TN 37659). Their stories have given us story ideas and shown us ways to enhance our own family storytelling tradition.

What chores did you have to do when you were a child?

- Which chores did you enjoy doing?
- Which did you have to do every day?
- Which were the ones you had to do only occasionally?
- What was the chore you absolutely hated doing?
- Did you ever refuse to do your chores?
- How did your responsibilities change as you got older?

You can tell your grandchildren what we call "grits" stories. On one of Kathryn Tucker Windam's storytelling tapes, she talks about how her mother fixed grits every morning for breakfast. She recounts all the different ways grits could be fixed. She talks for five or six minutes about grits, and in doing so gives the listener a flavor of her life as a child in the South.

A "grits" story is not so much a true story with a plot as it is a collection of interesting facts, thoughts, and memories about a subject from your childhood experience. Such details and description can give the whole family fascinating insights into your life and experiences.

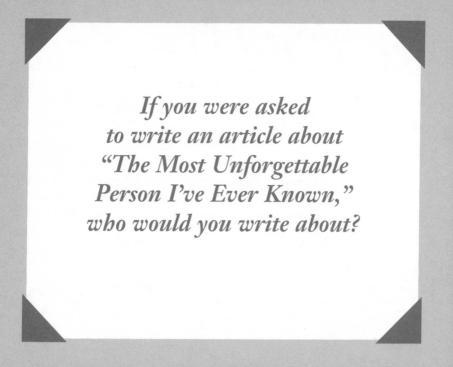

*If you were asked
to write an article about
"The Most Unforgettable
Person I've Ever Known,"
who would you write about?*

- How did you meet this person?
- How old were you at the time?
- What made that person unforgettable?
- Now tell about someone who was your hero.
- Or tell about the oldest person you ever met.

Stories reach past our minds and into our hearts. They bring us up close to the situation, so we feel the feelings and identify with the story's characters. Stories bypass misunderstanding or hurt feelings and bridge the gap between listener and teller. When the stories are told by grandparents about our families, they reinforce our sense of family identity, bolster self-esteem, and define our values.

Setting Up a Storytelling Session

Family storytelling in this day and age seldom just happens. So we'd like to offer a few suggestions and guidelines for scheduling a grandparent storytelling session. Because so many of us have lost the habit of family storytelling, it may take a little work and preparation to re-establish this family ritual. But it will be well worth the effort involved.

The FIRST STEP, if you are a grandparent, is to talk with one of your children and ask for his help in organizing this. If you are a parent who wants to get this started between your parents and your children, talk to the grandparents and ask for their cooperation. Assure them that you want to hear their memories.

The SECOND STEP is to set up a time and place. Invitations (at least informal ones) are in order. For example, let everyone know that after dinner on Sunday, Grandmother will be telling about her childhood. If other people know what to expect, they can look forward to it and will not feel awkward that day. Others may even bring their own questions to ask, or think of a story they want to hear again.

The THIRD STEP is to give the session a focal point. For example, the grandparent could select ten or twelve old photographs to talk about. Pictures are an excellent way to get the conversation started. And looking for the photos, in advance, gets the grandparent thinking about her past and the events that surrounded the taking of the pictures.

Or, instead of photos, you could plan to begin with a grandparent answering several questions related to a single theme. Choose a few from the story-starter questions in this book. When the grandparent knows ahead of time some of the things she's going to be talking about, she is better able to gather her thoughts and feel more comfortable from the outset.

The FOURTH STEP of preparation is to assign roles for the session. You could have three people with predetermined responsibilities. The first is the grandparent, who understands that it is her job to tell her memories. The second is a facilitator, whose job it is to get the session going and to keep it moving with added questions. The third person should be in charge of videotaping—something I strongly recommend.

Getting the Session Started

On the day of the storytelling session, the facilitator should gather everyone into a room where the grandparent can be seated comfortably, and where everyone can see and hear. Give the group a chance to talk and relax a little as they're settling in. After a few minutes of this, the facilitator should introduce the storytelling with a simple statement, such as, "I've asked Grandfather to tell us about his brothers and sisters" (or whatever the starting theme is going to be).

Now the facilitator becomes an active listener. This person can prod the grandparent with questions to help keep the storytelling going and on track. The story-starter questions (both those in big type and the follow-up questions in smaller type on opposite pages) can be used or serve as models for your own family questions. (This is true whether you set up a scheduled storytelling session like we're suggesting here, or you just want to use our questions to give you ideas for more informal conversations between family members from two or more generations.)

Each family will need to set its own pace. But don't plan for any structured storytelling to last more than an hour. When the stories seem to be winding down, the facilitator should bring things to a close.

*Locate ten to twelve
photographs that illustrate
some of your earliest memories.
Show the photographs
and talk about them.*

As each photo is shown, tell its story, answering such questions as:

- What are the names of the people or animals in this picture?
- When was it taken? Where?
- Who took the photo?
- Was this taken on a special day—a birthday, holiday, or trip?
- What house did you live in at the time this was taken?
- What else do you remember about this day?

Photographs serve as wonderful keys to unlock the doors to our memories. For these next few story-starter questions, we suggest using photographs to start the sharing process. If the grandparent telling the stories does not have photographs to illustrate any of these points, the questions can be answered and stories told from memory alone.

*Tell about your early memories
of your parents.*

If possible, illustrate your story with photographs of your parents as young people or children.

- How old was your mother when you were born? Your father?
- Tell their full names. Who were they named after?
- What work did your parents do?
- What did you enjoy doing with your parents? What didn't you enjoy?
- In what way was your mother different from any other mother you knew? Your father?
- What did your parents do with you that you promised you would do with your children?

Each grandparent storytelling session can have a different focus. The focus might be a specific era of life: earliest memories; school memories; the teenage years; courtship and marriage. Or you can tell about a specific day in your life: the daily routine, type of food eaten, etc. Photographs from each era (if available) can serve as a powerful memory aide, and an easy way to get the stories rolling.

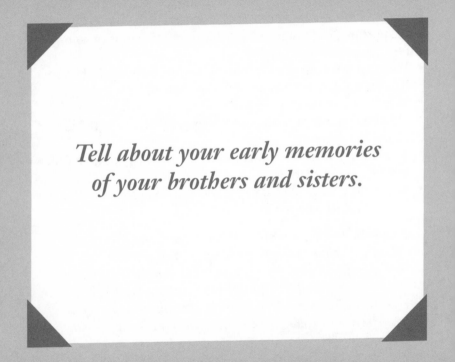

*Tell about your early memories
of your brothers and sisters.*

- If possible, illustrate the story with photographs of your siblings at different ages.
- Where did you fit in your birth family? Which brothers or sisters were older? By how many years? Which were younger? How much younger?
- Do you remember when your younger siblings were born? Tell about that memory.
- Which of your brothers or sisters did you go places or do things with? Tell us about an adventure—or misadventure—you had with that sibling.

Sometimes a single photograph or question will suggest story after story. Sometimes you may talk about a photo or particular memory for a minute or so and be done with it. Let each story take as long as it seems natural for it to take and for as long as the listeners have questions they want to ask.

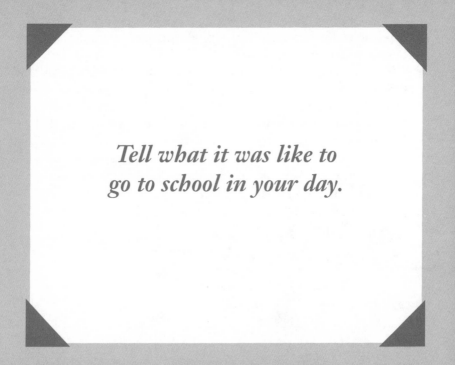

Tell what it was like to go to school in your day.

If you have them, gather photographs that illustrate your school experience. As you show each photo, answer such questions as:

- How old were you when you started school?
- Tell about your first day at school.
- What was the name of the first school you attended?
- How long did you go there?
- What are the names of any schoolmates pictured here?
- What did you do before school each day? After school?
- Do you remember a favorite teacher? What was his name? Why did you like him?
- How many rooms were there in your school? How many classes?
- Tell about a time when you got into trouble at school.
- Which subjects did you like? Which did you dislike?

A Bottle of Ink

I remember listening to my father tell stories about his childhood. One story that I retell to my children is the story of his first day of school. This is how I tell it to my children:

When my daddy was five years old, his mother walked him to the door of the school and said good-bye. He knew how to get to his classroom. But he decided to explore the school instead. He wandered around looking in this door and then that door, until he found a room where there wasn't anyone. He had found the teacher's dormitory. In those days the teachers lived in a room attached to the back of the school. And that was the room your granddaddy had found.

Now, in that room there was a couch, chairs, and a great big table. And in the middle of that table was a bottle of ink. That was where the teachers sat to grade their papers. And they used old-fashioned pens that had to be dipped into an ink pot.

Well, your grandaddy decided to play with that ink. And . . . he

got some ink on the table. And . . . on the chairs. And . . . more on that couch. He probably got some on the floor. And don't you just imagine that while he was doing it, he probably got some all over his clothes?

He kept playing with that ink until he heard a sound in the doorway. He looked up . . . and there was . . . the principal! Mr. Hicks had heard noise coming from the teacher's room and had come to investigate.

There, in the middle of the room, surrounded by ink, and covered with ink, was Charles Columbus Shaw!

Mr. Hicks grabbed your granddaddy—by whatever part of his arm had the least amount of ink on it—and walked him down the hall, out the door of the school, down the street, and all the way home. He knocked on the door (*knock, knock*) and told Mama Shaw that Charles needed to stay home and wait another year to start school. And he did.

Oh, how my children and I laugh at that story! But in hearing it my children come to know several things: We are a family that loves children even when they are rascals. We are a family willing to forgive and continue to love. We tend to be adventuresome and curious. And we value education.

That story passes along those values much more effectively than any lecture could ever do. And in the telling my father could laugh at the humiliation he felt at the time. In spite of his initial setback in education, he went on to finish school, college, and seminary.

*Collect photographs of trips
that you took when you were young.
Tell about one of those trips.*

- Tell the names of the people in the pictures.
- How old were you when you made this trip?
- Who went with you?
- Where did you go? Tell about what you saw there.
- How did you travel?
- What was fun about the trip? What wasn't fun?

> *If the stories seem to be winding down, or if you are getting tired, bring the session to a close. Some grandparents like to have a ritual closing: a song, a prayer, hands around a circle. Or you may close by hugging your grandchildren. Choose an ending that you are comfortable with.*
>
> *And don't be surprised if, once you have stopped telling stories, your children and grandchildren begin to tell stories themselves.*

*Tell a story of something
that happened on your birthday.*

If you have photographs of birthday celebrations, use them to begin your story.
- How old were you that year?
- Did you ever have a birthday party?
- What happened that day?
- Is there someone in the pictures whom you have not seen in years?
- Tell about a memorable birthday present you received.

One African proverb says, "When a knowledgeable old person dies, a library disappears." We preserve some of our personal "library" when we tell our grandchildren stories about our life experience.

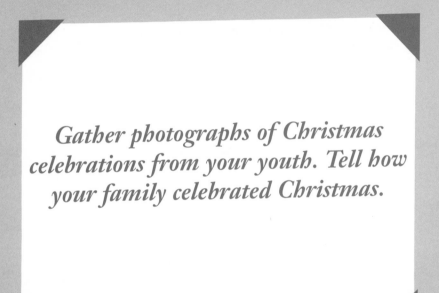

Gather photographs of Christmas celebrations from your youth. Tell how your family celebrated Christmas.

- How old were you in this Christmas photograph?
- What Christmas gift do you remember receiving on this day? Which do you remember giving?
- What Christmas traditions did your family have? Did you adopt some of those traditions for your family when you had children? Which ones?
- How did your family get and decorate their Christmas tree?
- What is the most special Chrismas gift you remember getting (or giving) as a child?

Grandpa and the Barn

This has always been one of our favorite Grandpa Lewis stories. Since his death, we tell it to his great-grandchildren. Not all of our children remember their great-grandfather, but they love to hear his story as we retell it.

The story I am telling you happened in December 1919. In fact it happened the day after Christmas that year.

On that day, a young farmer named Fred Lewis got up early in the morning, before it was even light outside—just the way he got up early every morning, the way farmers have gotten up before dawn for years and years. And he headed out to the barn to milk his cows.

That Fred Lewis was your great-grandpa Lewis. Grandpa lived in the same house, across the driveway from Uncle Leon and Aunt Mary's house, where he lived until he died. That was the same house he and his parents built when they moved to Coleman, Michigan, in 1900 when he was six years old.

On the day I'm telling you about, his parents didn't live there anymore. Grandpa lived there with his wife. Do you remember her name? (*Emma*) And their two year old son. What was his name? (*George*) And Emma was nine months pregnant with their second child. She had that baby two days later. Who did that turn out to be? (*Grandpa!*)

You're right. They had a baby boy, and they named him Ralph Loren Lewis. And he grew up to be your grandpa.

But on the day I'm telling you about, he hadn't been born yet. His mama and big brother George were fast asleep in the bedroom. And his daddy was out in the barn, getting ready to milk the cows.

As Grandpa Lewis reached to get the milking pail, he heard a voice in the barn. And the voice said, "Go back to the house!"

Now, Grandpa Lewis was *not* the sort of man that usually heard voices. And he certainly wasn't the kind of person who would do what some voice might tell him to do. So Grandpa thought, *I just came from the house! Why would I go back now?* And he turned around to get the milking stool.

He heard the voice again. "Go back to the house!"

Grandpa looked around to see where that voice might be coming from. He didn't see anyone or anything and, again, he thought, *I just came from the house. I don't want to go back there now.* And he set the milking stool down next to the first cow and took his seat.

And the voice came again. "GO BACK TO THE HOUSE!" And that time, Grandpa decided, all of a sudden, that he'd better listen to that voice. And he jumped up in such a hurry to go back to the house that he kicked that milking stool up against the side of the stall. *Whomp!*

And the voice added, "Take that milking pail with you." So Grandpa grabbed the bucket and lit out running for the house.

Now back in 1919, there was a well between the barn and the house. They took down the pump and covered the well over before any of you children were born.

On the day I'm telling you about, that well was there. And beside the well was a great big old rain barrel, full of water.

As Grandpa ran across that yard he looked up. There, in the window to the kitchen, he saw flames! As he ran past that barrel, he dipped the milk pail he was carrying into that barrel without ever stopping. He ran on to the house with a full bucket of water.

When he reached the kitchen, he saw fire coming from the flue pipe of the old wood cookstove, and a sheet of flame was spreading across the ceiling above the stove. Grease that had splattered from the stove onto the wall and ceiling had caught fire. At the end of the kitchen cabinet was a towel rack. Grandpa grabbed the towel off that rack, dipped it into the water, and standing on a kitchen stool, he wiped that fire out with that wet towel. He was able to put out that fire in just a few seconds.

Emma and little George kept right on sleeping. And two days later, that baby boy was born. And they named him Ralph. And Ralph grew up to be a man and met a woman named Margie Miller. They fell in love and got married. Their first baby was a boy and they named him . . . What? (*Gregg*) And that baby grew up and he met a woman named . . . What? (*Debi*) They fell in love and got married. What do you think they named their children? (*Andrew, Matthew, Lisette, Benjamin, and Jonathan*)

When Grandpa used to tell your daddy and me this story, he would shake his head and say, "This house was old and dried out, even when Ralph was a baby. It would have gone up in flames in just a few minutes if I hadn't come back to the house! If I hadn't brought the bucket, I wouldn't have had time to even run back and get it. Emma and George would never have woken up until it was too late."

Your great-grandpa Lewis always told us that he believed the voice in the barn was the voice of God. He believed that God wanted Emma and George to live and for that baby to be born. Who are some of the people we love who wouldn't have lived if Grandpa hadn't listened to the voice in the barn? (*And my children and I list them. If we remember them all, the list is fifty-three names long!*)

Just think how sad it would have been if I had grown up and there hadn't been your daddy for me to fall in love with! No Andrew, no Matthew, no Lisette, no Benjamin, no Jonathan. I sure am glad Grandpa Lewis listened to the voice of God in the barn that morning seventy-five years ago.

*Tell about the pets you had
when you were young.*

- Show a photo of that pet, if you have one.
- How old were you when you got this pet (or animal)?
- Tell about the day you got it. From whom or where did you get it? What was the occasion?
- Were you the one who fed it?
- Describe this animal's personality. Was it shy or friendly? Did it get into fights or was it picked on by other animals?
- How did you lose it? Did it die? How?

Tell grandparent stories at large family gatherings. When other family members are present who also remember the people and places of your past, you can jog each other's memories. And since no two people tell the same story about the same event, your children and grandchildren will enjoy hearing two sides to the same story.

*What sports did you play
when you were young?*

- If you have photographs of yourself playing sports, show those pictures and tell about them.
- How old were you when you played this sport? For how many years did you play?
- What position did you play?
- Who else was on the team? Were any of them your friends?
- Tell about the coach. Did you like or admire him? Why or why not?
- Was there ever a time when you were the team hero? Tell about that. Was there ever a time when you let your team down?

Have someone videotape your grandparent storytelling sessions, if at all possible. Such tapes are a valuable gift to your family. Copies can be sent to family members who were unable to come. And in watching the videotape, grandparents may remember more details to add to the story later.

*Tell about the first time
you remember riding
somewhere in a car.*

- Who did the car belong to?
- Who did the driving? Who else was in the car with you?
- What was the occasion for the ride?
- How old were you at the time?
- Describe the car's model, make, and color.
- Now tell about the first car your family owned. What was the model, make, and color? How old were you when you got it?
- Now tell about the first time you flew in an airplane or took a trip by train or bus.

Grandparents can vary in age from forty years old to a hundred. Whether or not these questions are pertinent for you will depend on your age and experience. Skip over the ones that do not apply to you.

*What movies did you see
when you were a child?*

- Tell about your favorites.
- What do you remember about the early days of television?
- Which shows were your favorites?
- When was the first time you saw a TV?

What are the three biggest ways life is different now than the way it was when you were young?

According to the National Storytelling Association: "Throughout history, storytelling has been as vital as life itself. Even today, people in every culture use storytelling to record and express the trials, joys, and challenges of their daily lives. Through storytelling, they give voice to traditions and values and create an oral history that can help to guide the next generation. . . . America's own rich oral tradition has grown quiet in recent years. But as the tumult of contemporary life threatens to overtake us, more and more people are awakening to the rewards and pleasures of storytelling."

Join the trend. Make a difference by telling stories.

Tell about your ethnic heritage.

- Did your family come to America from somewhere else?
- From where and how recently? How did they arrive? Where did they settle?
- What were the reasons for their coming?
- What hardships did they encounter before, during, or after their immigration?
- What injustice or prejudice did they encounter?
- How far back can you trace your ancestry?

Who was your favorite singer when you were young? What do you remember about listening to his music?

- What were your favorite songs?
- Did you ever see him in person? Tell us about that day.
- Did you see the Beatles on the Ed Sullivan show?
- What do you remember about Elvis?

> *Grandparents telling their own stories can be invaluable. But there is also often a place (and sometimes a need) for parents, or others, to retell those stories. Your adult children can retell your stories to your grandchildren, if you do not see your grandchildren often. And, of course, I retell my father's stories to my children, because he is no longer alive to tell them himself.*

Who was your favorite major-league baseball player or team? Tell about attending, watching, or listening to a memorable game.

- Did you collect baseball cards? Tell about that.
- Tell about getting an autograph from a ballplayer or from someone else.
- Tell about your sports heroes.

- Who was the most famous person you ever saw or met? Tell about that day.
- Tell about someone who lived in your town who was glamorous or impressive or a "big shot."

*Tell about the most exotic place
you ever traveled to.
Then tell about a place
you wish you could have traveled to.*

When you are telling stories to your grandchildren, tell them how old you were at the time and where you were. Include the names of the people in your story and how you were related to them. Describe what people and places looked like. Such details add flavor to your story and give the listener a frame of reference. Details enable your children and grandchildren to visualize the people and places of your past.

Tell what you remember about the day men first walked on the moon.

Or pick one of these historical events and tell how it impacted your life. What do you remember about:

- The day Pearl Harbor was bombed.
- The day you heard about Nagasaki or Hiroshima.
- D-Day in World War II.
- The day President John Kennedy was shot.
- The day Dr. Martin Luther King was killed.
- The day the U.S. pulled out of Vietnam.
- Where were you when you heard the news?
- Who were you with?
- How did you react?
- What happened the rest of that day?
- Did this event affect your life in any way?

Tell about the first U.S. president that you remember.

- What did your parents have to say about the president?
- Who was the first president for whom you voted?
- What issues made you decide to vote for him?
- What person, or people, influenced you in that election?

Once your family realizes how much fun grandparent stories can be, you will find yourself telling stories at most family gatherings. Don't hesitate to tell stories to one or two grandchildren alone, or in small groups, as well as at larger family get-togethers.

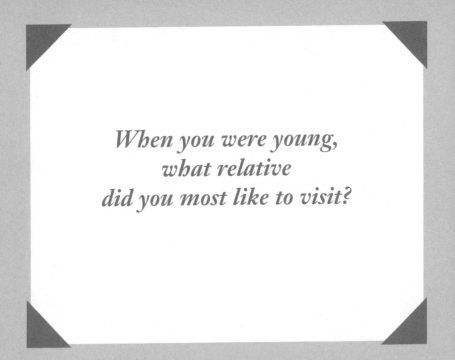

*When you were young,
what relative
did you most like to visit?*

- Tell about her. What was her name? How was she related to you?
- How often were you able to visit?
- What did you like best about the visits?
- What would you do during the visits? Did you eat special foods?
- Do you remember what that house smelled like?

Often people tend to tell about what they remember seeing in the past. Think about the other four senses. Remember what smells, sounds, and tastes you associate with each memory. How did someone or something feel to the touch? Sensory details add texture and flavor to stories.

Describe the first church you remember attending.

- Who took you to church?
- What denomination was it?
- Do you remember a sermon or Sunday school lesson?
- Tell about something funny you saw happen in church. Or tell about the time you misbehaved in church.
- Describe attending a wedding or a funeral in that church.
- What songs do you remember from church or Sunday school? Can you still sing them?
- Do you remember making personal decisions about your faith? Tell about those.

Story Starter

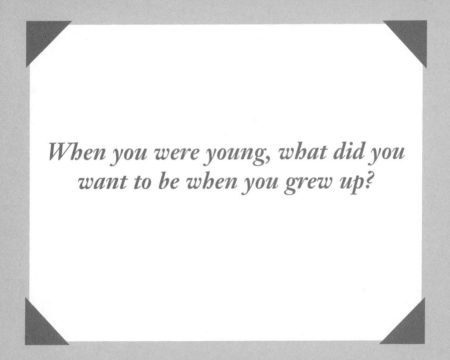

When you were young, what did you want to be when you grew up?

- How did that change as you grew older?
- Are there ways in which that imagined career compares with what you actually did later on in life?
- Tell about your first paying job.
- What was the worst job you ever had? The best? The most unusual? Explain.
- Have you ever changed jobs? Tell about that.

*Tell about the most
dangerous thing you ever did.*

- How old were you at the time?
- Who was with you?
- What made you decide to do what you did?
- Were you sorry afterwards?
- What happened as a result?
- Now tell the story of the day you did something outrageous.

What was the saddest day you remember from your childhood?

- What happened to make you sad?
- How did that day resolve itself?
- Now tell about an incident when you were frightened or embarrassed.
- And tell a story about a time you remember succeeding and feeling proud.

Tell about a time when you made someone very angry.

- Was the person involved a friend, parent, or sibling?
- What had you done?
- Were you sorry for what you did?
- Would you have done it again, if you could have?
- Now tell about the time you were so mad you wanted to strangle someone.

Don't let yourself feel pressured to answer a question that makes you feel uncomfortable. If such a question arises, simply say, "Let's leave that question for another time." And then move the conversation into a different direction.

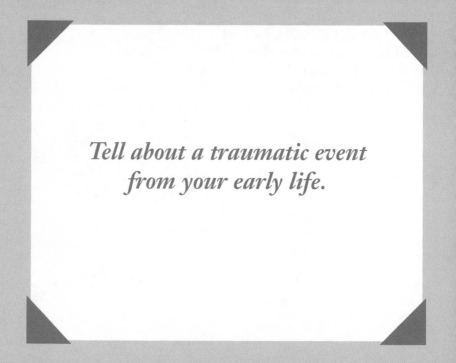

Tell about a traumatic event from your early life.

- Did you ever experience a tornado, flood, or other natural disaster?
- Do you remember the loss of a loved one?
- Did you survive a serious automobile accident?
- Did you ever suffer from a serious illness?
- How did that trauma influence who you are?

Did you ever run away from home?
Or at least think about it?
Tell us about that day.

Tell the stories of your failures as well as your successes. Stories of sadness and hardship give children a new perspective. They see how their grandparents faced troubles and triumphed, lived through sadness and found happiness again. Stories about your mistakes, weaknesses, and failures teach children about forgiveness and fortitude. Such stories enable our grandchildren to know us and at the same time allow us to feel truly known and loved. These stories revealing your humanness can be the most inspiring and encouraging stories you can tell.

Take the risk. Your family may bless you for your honesty.

Tell about a time when you deliberately misbehaved or disobeyed your mother or father.

- What were you thinking at the time?
- Who found you out and how were you discovered?
- How old were you?
- How were you disciplined?

Down by the River

One day my father, Charles, his brother James, and their mother, Mama Shaw, sat reminiscing about their past, while my brother Terrell videotaped. Note how each adds his or her part to the whole story. Terrell started the session off by saying, "Daddy, tell us about the river" (the Yellow River near Milstead, Georgia, where my father grew up).

Oh, that river! Mama, remember? Every time we got out of the yard, Mama would say, 'Ya'll better not go down by that river! I'll find it out! I'll send your father after you.' Oh, course, if she did send him after us, he'd find us."

"I don't know how ya'll lived to be grown!" Terrell laughed.

"Oh, he found us on the river many times," Charles continued.

"He even found us at Stone Mountain that time," James added. "We went all the way to Stone Mountain. And he found us. We even went on side roads—we weren't on one of the main roads."

"And he came driving up. He found us," Charles said.

"Of course that one time that Terry is interested in, we went to the river after we'd been to the golf course. We hadn't gotten a job caddying. All the other boys got the available jobs. So we decided to go to the river. When we got down there, the river was full of boys. You'd never seen it so—it was just full. James and I stripped off and jumped in that river.

"We swam across. The river was calm. On the other side you could mire up knee deep in sand. But where the river made the bend, it had washed out around the bank. It was deep. The only way to get out was to swim over to a low hanging limb—a root— and climb up on the root to get out. Well, we played there and time passed. Suddenly, there wasn't anybody there. Just me and James."

"And the water was rising!" added James.

"Yes, the river was rising and got muddy. We started back. I swam across and caught the root. I was pulling myself out and looked back. I didn't see James! I kept calling and finally his head came up out of the water. I said, 'James, come on!' He said, 'I can't!'"

"I turned loose of the root and went back and got him. I pulled him across that stretch. It's a wonder we didn't both drown. But, anyhow, we got over there and I helped him get up on that root and get out. And I got out.

"Well, his clothes were back way over, back toward the golf course. Mine were right on the bank. While we were standing there dressing, would you believe, the wind blew a tree over and it fell between us? Right between us! I had to climb over it—right through the limbs—to get to where James was."

"It was lightning—big clap of lightning—and the tree fell," James interjected.

"That's right. Sure was," Charles agreed. "I don't know if the lightning hit the tree or what."

"I wondered if the lightning hit it or the wind," James said. "But it fell!"

"It sure did!" Charles agreed. "And that's the same day that Hub Doyle told on us!"

James picked up the narrative. "He was going up the track and leaned out the train window. 'I see you boys, and I'm gonna tell your daddy on you,' he said."

"Who was Hub Doyle?" Terrell asked.

"He was the engineer of the old Milstead dinky," Charles said. "We had to cross the railroad tracks on our way to get to the river. It ran between the golf course and the river. And he came along and hollered, 'Okay, boys, I know where you're going! You better get back. I'm going to tell your daddy!'"

"And you said, 'Well, we're caught anyhow. We might as well go ahead,'" James said to Charles. "'We can go on,' you said, 'it won't be any different. If we go back, he'll tell anyway.'"

"Charles, I'd be ashamed. Leading your little brother astray. You'd have felt bad if he'd really drowned that day!" his wife said.

"Oh, Grady (*my grandfather*) was the cause of a lot of the things they done," Mama Shaw said. "He'd tell the tale about the things that happened when he was a boy. And they'd follow him and do what he did. Ain't no telling what all he did."

"But it was fun growing up!" Charles concluded.

In today's global community, we are exposed to constant media portrayals of famous people: from presidents to rock stars; from accomplished athletes to jet-setting billionaires. These are the people our world deems "significant." And in comparison to the people who make the headlines, we often think of ourselves as insignificant. Particularly as we grow older and it becomes apparent that we will never make the cover of *People* or even the president of the company, it is easy to undervalue the contribution we have made to life. We forget that in God's plan we all have value. Family stories remind us of our own significance.

Describe the town or city you lived in.

- How big was it?
- What was the best part of growing up there? The hardest part?
- To what places in town do you remember going?
- What did you like about them?
- Tell about the first expedition you made into town, by yourself, or with another child.
- Did your town have parades or other celebrations? On what occasions?

*Tell how you met your spouse
and about when you decided you
wanted to marry that person.*

No two people remember the same event in the same way. One of my few memories of my own grandfather is of sitting on the floor beside him, with my cheek against his knee, listening to his stories. My sister Beth remembers his stories as well, but she remembers sitting on his lap.

In the same way, if you and your spouse tell the story of your courtship and marriage, you may remember such different details that you end up telling two very different stories. If your siblings are present, they will have their own memories of your relationship, and add to the story. A variety of viewpoints adds color and interest to any story.

The Elopement

In December 1987, Gregg videotaped his Grandma Miller telling the story of her marriage. She and Grandpa were married sixty-four years and eleven months. This was taped the first Christmas after Grandpa died.

Gregg started it off with, "A good place to start would be to talk some about the day you eloped with Grandpa. I'd like to hear that story again."

Well, it was on a Monday night. I told my mother that I wasn't feeling good. And, of course, she was always in sympathy with us when we didn't feel good. I'd been sleeping upstairs. But that night I slept downstairs, right around the corner from where she was sleeping.

"Before I went to bed for good, she told me to get up and shut the door. So I went and got a drink of water, and I turned the latch on the door, like I was shutting it. But I left it open. Wide open. This was the door that went out to the kitchen, and in from the kitchen to the living room. That's where I put my clothes. I always put them out for the next day's school. She didn't think nothing of that."

"How old were you?" Gregg asked.

"I'd have been eighteen in November. This was September the 20th. So that night, I heard her snoring. She had my sister Bernice; she was only a year old. She had Bernice in bed with her. And she was snoring. I thought she was asleep. But I didn't know for sure. So I got down on the floor. This was in the dining room where I was sleeping, and I got down on the floor, and got under the five-legged table, and I got stuck fast. I had an awful time getting out without making noise.

"She'd told me to shut the door, and I had already shut it halfway and then opened it, to make her think it was shut. Now I went into the living room where my clothes were, and I grabbed all my clothes and went barefooted down a half-mile to meet Jim, when he arrived at the end of the lane.

"When I got there, he was there. We both came at the same time. He marveled at that and so did I. We went on the other side of Whistler."

"How did you go? Did you have a car?" Gregg asked.

"Yes, he drove a car. And I put my shoes and stockings and clothes on. I didn't take time to get out of my bedclothes. He picked me up in my nightclothes!

"It was about two o'clock by the time we got to Columbus. And he had the tickets for the train ride to Cincinatti, and we went from there over to Covington. We was married in Covington."

"Because you could get married in Kentucky without your parents' signature?" Gregg asked.

"Yes, we told them we were of age. They accepted what we told them."

"How old was Grandpa then?" Gregg asked.

"Grandpa was twenty-one in March and I was lacking a little bit being eighteen."

"Grandpa had talked to your parents about marriage before that, hadn't he?" Gregg added.

"Oh, yes. And Mom said, 'Now, Jim, you wouldn't run off with her, would you?' And he said, 'I won't make you no promises!' So she didn't trust him. She didn't trust me out with him for four weeks before we was married. And he come there in the shade while I milked and waited on me. And I'd visit with him till way in the night. But Mom stayed around where she could see us.

"Now, two weeks after we was married, I went back to get some clothes of mine. And she throwed them out at me. But two weeks after that she was coming to see me. After two weeks she couldn't take it no more."

Did you do something when you were young that no one knows about? Is there something about you that would surprise us? Tell us about it.

Burned-Up Shoes

In June 1986, my father, Charles, his mother (we called her "Mama Shaw"), and his brother James were sitting around telling jokes and stories. On the spur of the moment, my brother Terrell got the camera out and started taping their reminiscing. The result is a gift of priceless value to those of us who loved to hear their stories, for my father died later that year. And Uncle James and Mama Shaw both died in 1993.

James started with, "Do you remember, Charles? When we'd just got brand-new tennis shoes and we went down there to the river and got them wet? We built a fire and was going to dry them out? And we burned them up!"

"Yep! We burned 'em up!" Charles laughed.

"Talk about scared to go home!" James said.

"Daddy got so mad, he exploded," Charles said. "And he said, 'You can't earn a living! If they don't wear them out, they burn 'em up!'"

"Shoot, we didn't get but one pair a year!" James said.

"Don't tell me that!" Mama Shaw protested. "Charles wore out a pair every three weeks! Grady was working a long time, a-raising up you boys."

"Oh, he was working six days a week in the mill," Charles added. "Five and a half days. And all the rest of the time until midnight in the barber shop."

"That was twelve hours a day!" James added.

"He would work eleven hours a day in the mill," Charles continued. "It really was twelve, 'cause he came home for lunch. His pay was eleven hours. And after six o'clock in the afternoon, he'd come running in and grab a bite and run to the shop."

"He'd stay out until one or two o'clock in the morning," James added.

"Right!" Charles agreed. "And on the weekends he'd work in the mill until twelve o'clock noon and come home. Then he brushed up and cleaned up and went to the barber shop."

"He was making about six dollars a week at that time," James added.

"Less than twenty cents an hour," Charles agreed. "I didn't get but twenty-five cents an hour when I went to work. Daddy was making less than that at the time."

What a memorable picture of life in the time of my grandparents! I gained respect for my grandfather, realizing how hard he had worked to give his five sons a good life! What a woman Mama Shaw had been, raising five rambunctious sons while her husband worked such long hours! How remarkable my father must have been to finish high school (unusual for mill-town boys), answer the call of the ministry, go to college in another state, and then go on to seminary. I am so grateful to have that videotape, to help me remember and for my children to see.

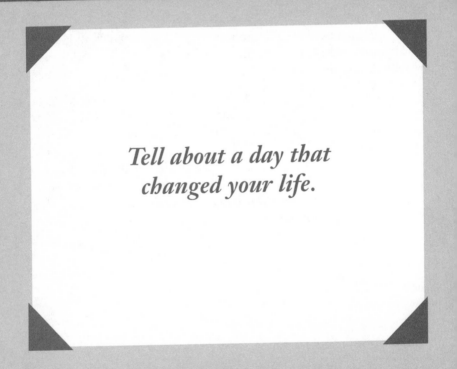

Tell about a day that changed your life.

- What happened?
- How old were you?
- Where did this happen?
- What made it so important to your life?
- Did you have a decision to make?
- How was your life different after this day?
- Did those changes make you happy or sad?
- Tell about the day you decided to become a Christian.

Everyone has turning points in their lives. A decision must be made: who to marry, what career to pursue, if and where to go to college, whether or not to move. Sometimes the turning point is out of our control. We are fired from our job. Or the person we want to marry says good-bye or dies. Because these days are crucial to who we are as people, they tend to stand out in our memory. Stories about such crucial days help the listeners understand how we became the people we are today.

*Tell about leaving home
for the first time.*

- Why did you leave?
- Where did you go?
- How long before you returned home for a visit?
- Did you ever move back home? For how long?
- Tell about your experience in the military.

"Did I Ever Tell You About . . ."

Family values—it's been one of the hottest of political hot buttons in recent years. Definitions vary. But almost everyone agrees his own family's values are important.

Traditionally, storytelling has been one of the primary means by which family identity and family values have been conveyed from one generation to another. It has also helped children gain a sense of belonging and enhanced self-esteem. Today, in a culture marked by so many fractured family relationships, and in a mobile society that has eroded our concept of the extended family, storytelling holds real promise for strengthening ties too easily broken or lost. And when it's incorporated into the routine of family life, it can lay the foundation for a lifetime of open, honest communication between generations.

We trust that as you have been reading this book, you have begun experimenting with family stories of your own. We want to assure you that as you continue your adventure in storytelling, you will discover more and more stories which help define your family as uniquely your own.

And we hope you have been having fun. For a grandparent's storytelling should be enjoyable—both for the elder doing the telling and all those who listen. If it's not fun, relax and slow down. It often takes time for stories to come together, for families to develop the habit of telling stories.

But as you begin to incorporate storytelling into your time with your family, it can indeed become a habit, woven into the very fabric of your relationships with each other. And the more family stories you tell, the easier it will become to do and the larger role grandparents and grandparents' stories will play in the life of your family.

Soon the children in your family will be clamoring for storytime. And grandparents will find themselves regularly asking, "Did I ever tell you about . . ."

Enter the Creating Family Memories Contest!

Do you have a family story to share? It could get you published! Or send you on a family vacation of a lifetime!

Here's How. Write out your favorite family story and mail it to the address below. Your story will be judged on its originality and on how well the event created a lasting memory or drew your family together. The story must be original and not previously published, typed or neatly handwritten, and 500 words or less.

The Prizes. The ten best stories will be published in *Christian Parenting* ($100 value). Grand prize is a six-day, five-night family vacation for four to anywhere in the continental United States. The contest is cosponsored by USAir and Holiday Inn.

Mail in your story with your name, address, and phone number to: Creating Family Memories, Attn. Betty Wood B16, Zondervan Publishing House, Grand Rapids, MI 49530.

The Official Rules. No purchase necessary. Ten winners will be published in *Christian Parenting* magazine ($100 value). One grand prize consists of six days, five nights at a Holiday Inn, round-trip airfare on USAir, rental car, and $200 spending money, for a total $2,500 value. No cash substitute. Entries must be received by March 31, 1995. Judging will be conducted by a panel, and its decisions shall be final. Sponsor not responsible for lost or damaged mail. Taxes are winners' responsibility. All entries become the property of sponsor. The contest is open to residents of the United States, 21 years and older. All prizes will be awarded. Employees or their family members of Zondervan, Family Bookstores, HarperCollins, or their advertising affiliates may not enter. A list of prize winners may be obtained after July 31, 1995 by sending a self-addressed, stamped envelope to the address listed above.